W9-AXL-468

Bouncy

The Basketball That Couldn't Bounce

Crosby,

Jim [signature]

This book is dedicated to our children,
Jennifer, Ethan, Jaret and Parker.

BOUNCY: THE BASKETBALL THAT COULDN'T BOUNCE
Copyright © 2020 by Jim and Brenda Jones
Published by Jim Jones Enterprises LLC, Avon Lake, OH

All rights reserved. Printed in the United States of America. No part of this book may be used or reproduced in any manner whatsoever without written permission except in the case of brief quotations embodied in critical articles or reviews. This book is a work of fiction. Names, characters, businesses, organizations, places, events and incidents either are the product of the author's imagination or are used fictitiously. Any resemblance to actual persons, living or dead, events, or locales is entirely coincidental.

For information regarding permissions email: JimBballJones@gmail.com or visit JimBasketballJones.com

ISBN: 978-1-7350356-2-8

First Edition: September 2020

Bouncy

The Basketball That Couldn't Bounce

Jim and Brenda Jones

Bouncy the Basketball was stuck in a bush. He had goosebumps from the cold, wet drizzle.

He moved a little to scratch an itch and fell out onto the grass.

Whew! That felt better.

He wondered, "How did I end up here? In the dark? In the rain?"

Bouncy's day had started out fine. He was fresh and brand new, in his box at a toy store.

A lady picked him up and took him to a clerk. She asked, "Do you gift wrap? It's for my son Derick. It's his birthday!"

The clerk took Bouncy's box and taped it up with blue paper and a bow. He couldn't see out!

Later, Derick ripped
off Bouncy's paper.

He shouted,
"A basketball! Thank you, Mom!"
Bouncy thought, "Oh, boy! This is going to be fun!"

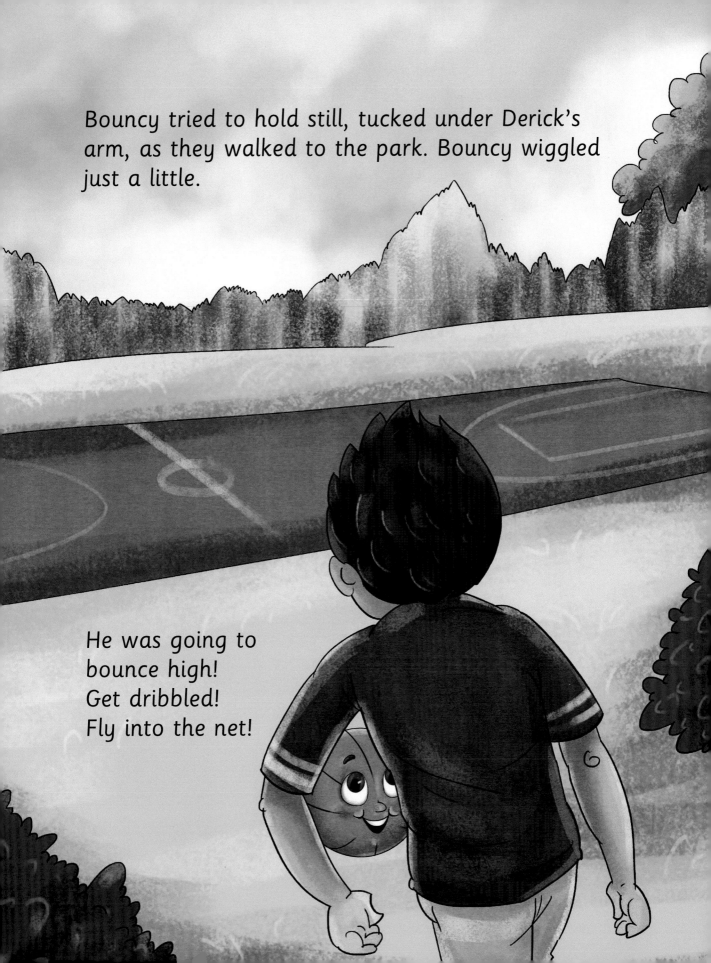

Bouncy tried to hold still, tucked under Derick's arm, as they walked to the park. Bouncy wiggled just a little.

He was going to bounce high! Get dribbled! Fly into the net!

But then, something terrible happened. Derick tossed Bouncy and Bouncy didn't bounce. Derick said, "This ball is no good! It's soft! It's flat on one side!"

He gave Bouncy a big kick across the park and into the bush.

Bouncy thought Derick would come back. He would take him home and they would play.

Bouncy would sail up to the basket, bounce off the backboard and fly into the hoop.

But Derick never came back.

Bouncy had cried,
but now,
in the dark,
he was just wet
from the rain.

The next day was sunny and warm. Birds chirped. Children laughed and played. Bouncy rolled a little. He wanted to play, too.

Then it happened!
Bouncy noticed a boy running towards him.

Bouncy saw a twinkle in the boy's eyes. Should he risk it?
Should he talk to him?
Bouncy asked, "Do you want to play?"

The boy looked around.

Bouncy said, "Down here! It's me! Bouncy! Will you play with me?

The boy's eyes grew wide. He looked at Bouncy and Bouncy smiled.

The boy said, "You can talk?!!"

Talk? Bouncy had so much to say that he couldn't stop!

He found out that the boy's name was Cal. Bouncy told Cal how he wanted to

bounce!

To be

dribbled!

To fly into a **hoop!**

He told Cal the sad story of how he was kicked and left alone in the park.

Cal listened to Bouncy for a long time. Then he dropped Bouncy. Bouncy tried really hard to bounce, but he just did a belly flop. Cal picked him up and said, "Hmm... I don't think you were made to bounce.

But don't give up! You're the one and only you! I'll help you find what you can do!"

Bouncy and Cal went everywhere together.

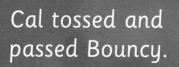

Cal tossed and passed Bouncy.

It was fun to feel that rush of air!

But Bouncy was still sad because he couldn't bounce. Cal said,

"Keep believing, Bouncy!

You're the one and only you! Soon we'll find what you can do!"

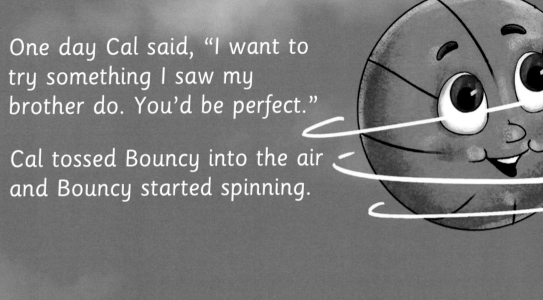

One day Cal said, "I want to try something I saw my brother do. You'd be perfect."

Cal tossed Bouncy into the air and Bouncy started spinning.

Cal landed Bouncy on the tip of his finger and Bouncy kept spinning. Bouncy shouted, "Wow! Look at me!" When Cal stopped, Bouncy felt a little dizzy, but he said, "Do it again!" Cal spun Bouncy again and again.

Cal said, "We did it, Bouncy! We just found what you can do!"

In the next days and weeks, Cal and Bouncy got better and better at spinning.

Cal spun Bouncy off his arms. He spun Bouncy off his forehead.

Cal and Bouncy showed off their spinning skills to kids in the park.

Bouncy *loved* to spin, but sometimes he still looked sadly at the basket.

One full moon night, Cal took Bouncy outside. He looked up at the basket and got a smile on his face.

Then with a twist, a spin and a
shout Bouncy went into the air
spinning faster than he'd ever
done before.

Balancing Bouncy on his finger, Cal ran
towards the basket. He jumped and tossed
Bouncy way up in the air.

Bouncy hit the backboard and went down into the net. "Woohoo!!!" Cal and Bouncy shouted for joy!

Bouncy didn't need to bounce! He could spin right into a basket!

Bouncy and Cal went everywhere, spinning and making kids smile. Bouncy was all smiles, too.

Now he knew what he could do! Bouncy was a trick basketball!

You are unique. You are important and you matter. Don't ever quit. Remember, you're the one and only you! There's something special you can do!

You can do it, my friend!

Jim Jones

You were born to sparkle! Believe, have hope and dream. Share your unique gifts with the world and in turn, you may help someone find theirs.

Brenda Jones

You have a special gift. Don't ever quit trying to find what you can do. Learn more about me and my really cool friends Yeti and Speedy at www.JimBasketballJones.com/Bouncy.

Your friend,

Bouncy

About the Authors

Jim "Basketball" Jones is a National Youth Motivational Speaker and Author with over 20 years as a professional school assembly speaker. With over 8,000 school assemblies performed, Jim is a leader in the school assembly and character education field.

Bring Jim to your school, group or organization for an Author visit or School Assembly. Find out how to schedule Jim at: www.JimBasketballJones.com. You can follow Jim on Facebook @JimBasketballJones and Twitter @JimBballJones

Brenda Jones, M. Ed, is an award winning educator (Franklin B Walters Award Recipient) with over 25 years of teaching experience. She is known for making learning magical and infecting her students with a love of reading. Her students love her weekly Facebook Live bedtime stories @Mrs.Jones Kindergarten. You can follow her on Twitter @KdngDisneyJones